THE TAIL
OF THE
TRINOSAUR

BM

The disappearance of great books is not a problem easily solved, and quite why Charles Causley's rollicking epic poem, *The Tail of the Trinosaur* fell out of print and out of fashion isn't clear. Sadly, this may have nothing to do with the quality of the work, and everything to do with the movements of capital between larger and smaller publishers.

But let's leave that to one side, and remember Charles and his poem. I met him on several occasions in his home in Launceston in Cornwall where he lived for virtually all his life. He was a modest, fun-loving man, full of wonder and wry amusement. I was particularly interested to find out that in his youth he had had what might be called leftish leanings, which may explain one or two things about our friend the Trinosaur. As a writer, Charles first made an impact in the 1950's with the publication and repeated anthologizing of his poem about a boy called Timothy Winters. Both the versification and the theme seemed to be at one and the same time, very modern and rather ancient. And this was Charles himself. All his life, he harnessed the traditional forms of English poetry to modern horses.

With the *Trinosaur* we have a tale that weaves several familiar images: expeditions to far-away places, the strange survival of ancient life-forms, dragons near villages, parish elders in a kafuffle, virgin sacrifice, alongside some newer ideas about saving rare species, preventing armed forces from mowing down what's in their sights. Running through these large images are dozens of smaller details that evoke a just-passed English life: Bill the boiler-man who sends the heating temperature sky-high, or the Victory Illuminated Fountain in the centre of the village. And there's something gloriously civic about the whole episode, with the involvement of mayors and committees and the like – a faint echo of the Pied Piper here, perhaps, though there's no fishy business with any mayoral double-dealing in the poem.

So what is it about? What's it for? Well, at one level,

it's a classic romp: the strange creature that comes to town, and is taken to be a threat – think King Kong, Godzilla and the rest. The twists that Charles gives this core story are that this menacing monster is no more than a clumsy vegetarian; she is distinctly unimpressed by a virgin coming to recite a self-sacrificial poem and will, in the end, beyond the end of the poem, almost certainly be the mate of a male. There are messages of a sort – people in authority bumble along, it's good not to exterminate rare species, the might of the army can be subverted. Much of the satisfaction of the piece, though, is to be found in the energy, variety and inventiveness of the versification. Here is a virtuoso poem, full of delights, corners, originalities and surprises. Please read this pleasure-loving romp out loud, with plenty of cod accents and ham gestures. Your audience awaits.

Michael Rosen

ABOUT CHARLES CAUSLEY

Charles Causley was born in Launceston, Cornwall in 1917, and aside from his naval service in World War II, lived there all his life. He left school at 15 and worked in a builder's office, playing the piano in a dance-band in the evenings, before serving during World War II in the Royal Navy. He then returned to Launceston, and worked until his retirement as a primary school teacher, publishing poetry, stories, hymns and plays and receiving many honours. Loved by his fellow poets, Charles Causley loved and understood children, and knew what they liked instinctively.

*The Tail of
the Trinosaur
is told in
24 shakes*

To Frances and Carey Tolchard

JANE NISSEN BOOKS
Swan House
Chiswick Mall
London W4 2PS

First published 1972 by Brockhampton Press
Published in Jane Nissen Books 2006

Printed and bound in Gateshead by Athenaeum Press

A CIP catalogue record of this book is available from the
British Library

ISBN 978-1-903252-23-9

The Tail of the Trinosaur

Charles Causley

Illustrated by
Jill Gardiner

Jane Nissen Books

Shake 1

In Dunborough town
   On the River Drown
      One morning in mild September,

On a day as fair
   Over Guildhall Square
      As anyone could remember,

While the folk all went
   On their business bent
      As they had since the days of the Briton,

And the cows all chewed
   And the pigeons cooed
      As when Domesday Book was written,

A VEHICLE bright
   With flashing light
      – To sirens screaming like a banshee –

Through the South Gate scraped
   As the people gaped
      And cried, excitedly, '*Can* she?'

And from Plymouth Dock
   As the Town Hall clock
      Emitted its usual quarter

There braked in the Square
    With a squeak of air
    A perfectly
            vast
        TRANSPORTER.

With a wondering sound
    As the crowds surged round
    It was plainer
        and plainer
            and plainer

That they couldn't decide
    Just what was inside
    The simply
        e n o r m o u s
        CONTAINER.

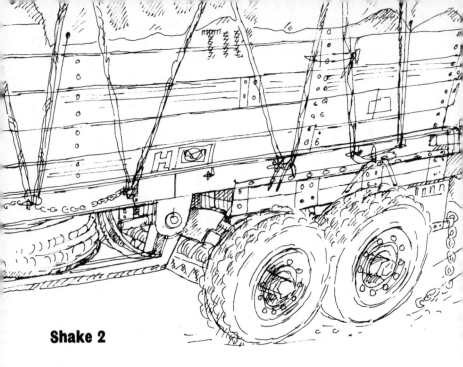

Shake 2

Then out of the cab swung the driver's mate
    Like an act at an open-air gala,
And the crowd gave a cheer that the Mayor could hear
    As he polished his chain in his Parlour.
'Dear me!' said His Worship. 'What *is* going on?
    I'd best put on my regalia,
For it might, by a fluke, be a Royal Duke
    Or a visiting Mayor from Australia.'

Up the Town Hall steps ran the driver's mate
    As the townsfolk tittled and tattled,
And he drew from his coat a delivery-note
    And the knocker he loudly rattled.
'Who's there?' said the Mayor as he opened the door
    By its medieval handle,
Then his jaw he dropped and his eyes he popped
    In the manner of a Roman candle.

For there THE MIGHTY TRANSPORTER stood
    And over the people towered,
Quite blocking the scene from the Castle Green
    To the bar of the 'Admiral Howard'.
And the Mayor (as he signed) looked quite nonplussed
    And claimed it was all a bungle.
'But it's marked on the freight,' said the driver's mate.
    'A PRESENT FROM THE AMAZON JUNGLE.'

Now the crate it stood a haystack high
    And its length was a hundred metres
And the Mayor turned as grey as a seaman may
    When he's gone and lost his neaters.*

Just as nobody knew just what to do
    And the children's lips looked quivery,

* A ration of neat rum.

Right up to the Mayor
                    drove
                              Postman Dare
With an air-mail,
            SPECIAL DELIVERY!
For a moment His Worship stood dumb and still
    As a stone Egyptian pharaoh,
Then he scratched his poll, said 'Bless my soul —
    It's
        a
            letter
                from
RIO DE JANEIRO.'

And a curious hush in quite a rush
    Fell over the whole assembly
As the Mayor began the letter to scan,
    His fingers distinctly trembly.

Then his frown was gone and his face it shone
    With a smile so reassuring,
And he said, 'Such a tale I'll now unveil
    As will send your spirits soaring,
Telling all and one of a Dunborough son
    In a lonely jungle-station,
And his GIFT of renown to his old HOME-TOWN
    That will make it the ENVY of the NATION.'

He could hardly hide a tear of pride
    And a couple of noisy swallows,
Then with manly zest he expanded his chest
    And read out the letter
                    as follows.

Shake 3

Mr Mayor,

As I sit in my cabin so small
On the banks of the Amazon River Where
green anacondas through forests crawl And
incredible butterflies shiver, Where boa constrictors
hang down from the trees On branches both
lower and upper To give the unwary a bit of a
squeeze And swallow him slowly for supper: As
high all around the brazil-wood ride The busy
humming-birds hurtle And there glitter and glide
on the evening tide The alligator and turtle Where
a million monkeys from bough to bough Like
woolly birds are zooming, And the jaguar trots
all covered in spots, And orchids rare are blooming;
When I've fried for my supper as evening falls
A plate of steak-armadillo, And my coffee is
drunk and I fall on my bunk — as soon as my
head's on the pillow, I dream every night of the
days long ago When Dunboro Town I would
wander, Never thinking one day I'd be far, far
away Exploring the Great Out Yonder. And when

I remember the deeds that I've done (To admit
it I'd once have been warier) It seems to me I
was certainly THE Most horrible boy in the area.
For I poured dirty water down Widow Brown's
flue, Dressed her donkey in silks and in satins,
And I painted each pew in the church with glue
One day before choral matins.

It was I who set fire to the robes of the choir
From the trebles right down to the basses, And the
water supply I coloured with dye On the day
of the Swimming Club Races. My collection of
fleas to the jumble sale I sent in a box
marked "Havanas", And I hung for a lark the
trees in the park With bunches of stolen bananas.

I filled up the seat of the magistrate's chair
With holly and thistles and prickles, And the lily-
white coat of the rectory goat I painted with
hammers and sickles.

But a time came at last when my boyhood was
past And those crimes in my throat they were
sticking, My remorse it was deep, I was losing my
sleep And my conscience was constantly pricking.
So a gift I decided to send to them all By which

they'd remember me sweetly, And I hunted
the points of the compass about For something
to fill the bill neatly, And imagine my pride (I'd
rejected the hide Of a mammoth and also a dino-
saur) When with fortune unique I found stuck
up a creek The world's weirdest wonder

a trinosaur !

As above me it leered I confess it appeared To be
not only living but kicking, And I haven't a
doubt that my eyes were both out Of my head with
astonishment sticking, For there's not much I've
missed as a naturalist In my travels to pole and
equator, But I solemnly swear of a creature so
rare I was never before the spectator. For millions of
years in the swamp it had laim More or less in the
same old position, All covered in goo of a horrible hue
That had kept it in splendid condition. Why, it scarcely
seemed dead! From its tail to its head It was perfect
in every feature, And in Dunborough's name I at
once staked a claim On that

truly
remarkable
creature.

Shake 4

So with tackle and with crane From the
place where it had lain We lifted it, as careful
as could be, And one Sunday afternoon On
a sort of a pontoon It was floated down the
river to the sea.
And the savage Indian tribes, Coffee-planters
and their wives In amazement held their hands
up to the sky As they stood upon the shore And
they saw that trinosaur Just like an ocean-
liner pass them by.
Now the size of this strange figure Was a circus-
tent's - or bigger - Though its stem and stern were
infinitely slender. Down its spine, like sugar-lum[p]
Ran a single row of bumps, Thus denoting that it
was of female gender. And it had a pair of eyes
Each a dustbin-lid in size In a head that was
the size of a small barque.
("Oh I'm glad," cried more than one, "Such
monster's dead and gone, For I wouldn't ca[re]

5/ to meet it after dark!") It had most un-
pleasant claws And the hungriest of jaws That
were ever seen in continent or ocean, But the
most astounding feature of this antiquated
creature Was its most amazing _mode of loco-
motion._

There were two legs at the front But its rear
was rather _blunt_ And was quite devoid of
limbs in every way, And it would have _scraped_
the floor And have made the trino sore Had its
tail not acted as a prop and stay.

So with many a start and stop, Half a leap
and half a hop, It had pranced around in prehistoric climes, Though the reason's pretty clear Why it grew
extinct, I fear, For it simply hadn't travelled with
the times.

When it reached the city docks It was packed in
such a box — The largest ever from the naval store—
That a thousand dockyard-maties Cried, "We don't

know WHAT that freight is For we've
never seen the like of it before!"

Then they lashed it to a raft Of consid-
erable draught And with a pair of tow-
ropes quite gigantic They secured it to
the stern Of the tug known as <u>The Tern</u>
That hauled it clean across the loud
Atlantic.

When I heard (while down in Chile)
It had reached the Isles of Scilly I at
once put pen to paper with its story,
For to reach its destination With no
word of explanation Would have
caused a fearful fuss and a furore.

Now to Dunborough and its folks,
To make up for my bad jokes, This

7/

trinosaur, in recompense, I send; And
it comes with love from one who prefers
to be anon. Which is why he simply

signs himself

A Friend

Shake 5

So with hammer and chisel and mallet and crow
    They cautiously cracked the container – and oh
With terror some trembled and awe they all cried
    When they first caught a glimpse of the creature inside.

From the tip of its tail to the top of its head
    They'd never seen anything like it, they said.
'We know,' cried the workmen, 'its life is long done,
    But it's all we can do not to down tools and run!'

Said the Mayor, 'Though it means that the rates are increased,
    We *must* build a Suitable Home for the beast
– As in London and New York and Paris you see 'em –
    A Dunborough Natural History Museum.

And before you said Alderney, Guernsey or Sark
    (Or Jersey, for that) down at Priory Park
The lorries arrived and the builders began
    On Sir Archibald Architrave's prize-winning plan.

The roof was a bubble that spun round about,
    The walls slanted inwards, the windows leaned out.
With colours astonishing it was a-shine,
    And practically everyone thought it divine.

But old Grannie Penney who lived by the river
  Said, 'Something about the place gives me a shiver.
That silly old kickshaw I simply can't bide
  Any more than the monster they're putting inside.

'I can't see the church-yard, it's ruined my view,
  My lights are all blocked and I think I shall sue,
My cat has had kittens, my dog's having fits,
  And the nerves of my budgie are bothered to bits.

'Quite up with that building I really am fed,
  It's more like a tumbledown aeroplane shed.
I'll move to my sister's in Abergavenny
  If fate don't move first,' grumbled old Grannie Penney.

'Each time that I shake out a duster or mat
   That beast makes me come over funny, that's flat.
And night after night when I go to my bed
   It seems to be *staring right at me*,' she said.

'I don't like the look that it's got in its eye
   (Although it's a dead 'un) – I just don't know why.
That creature means trouble! You'll all rue the day!'
   Said old Grannie Penney, '*so mark what I say.*'

Shake 6

BUT –

The hammers they rang
  And the saws they sang
    As the builders went through their paces,

And the steel and the glass
  Fairly jumped off the grass
    And into the proper places.

They struggled with struts
  And they juggled with nuts,
    And they bolted and braced and cleated,

Till at last with a cheer
(And a barrel of beer)
It was
Absolutely
finally
completed.

And right in the middle
   Stood the green and grinning trinosaur,
Its eye and coat a-gleaming
   As if it was in its prime,
For they'd scrubbed it
   And polished it
   As fine as you or I e'er saw
Till gone was every single speck
   Of tropic mud and slime.

Its shiny tail was slippery
   (You could have made a slide of it)
And imitation jungle trees
   Were built with finest art,
With lots of central heating
   At the front and back and side of it
To keep the creature cosy
   So it wouldn't fall apart.

And the Mayor and Corporation
 Very early took their station
  (Robed and ermined) as determined
   By the Dunborough Town Clerk,

And behind the Borough banner
In a very stately manner
They proceeded in procession
To the site on Priory Park.

There were guests — at least a score —
  And their morning coats they wore,
    Also shiny toppers, silver ties and spats,

And their wives (with spacious smiles)
  In the very latest styles,
    That included most extraordinary hats.

There was scarlet Admiral Bounty
  – Lord Lieutenant of the County –
    There were brownie guides and cub scouts standing steady,

And officials large and small
    Who'd come down from County Hall,
        And the Fire Brigade with engine at the ready.

As the Band made an assault on
  'Orb and Sceptre' (William Walton)
  And a set of variations
    On 'The Bonnie Brier Bush',

Crowds and crowds of people muttered,
And the flags and banners fluttered,
And the children got all cluttered,
And their parents murmured,
      'Ssh!'

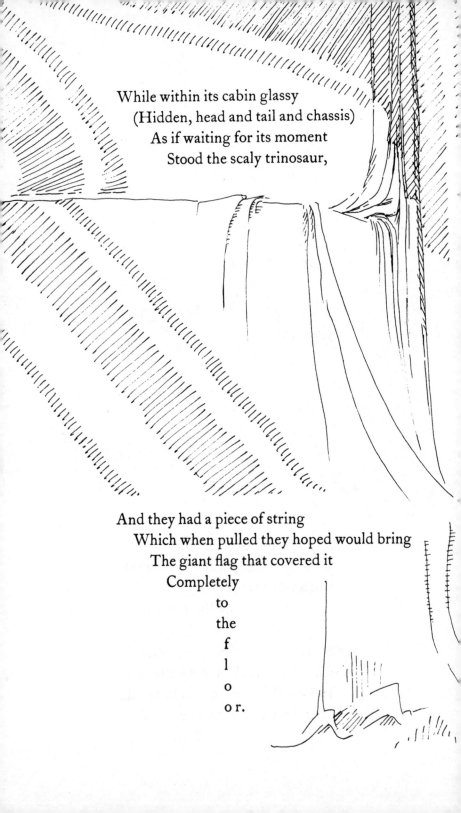

While within its cabin glassy
(Hidden, head and tail and chassis)
As if waiting for its moment
Stood the scaly trinosaur,

And they had a piece of string
Which when pulled they hoped would bring
The giant flag that covered it
Completely
to
the
f
l
o
o r.

Meanwhile from St. Mary's tower
   From a very early hour
      The ringers sounded out a happy peal,
And in accents proud, the Mayor
   Said, 'This building I declare
      Is quite open, and my joy I can't conceal.'

Then he pressed a little switch
   And without the slightest hitch
      As the sort of silence fell one can't ignore,

Down the covers fell so neat
From its head right to its feet
And revealed to all the world
THE
TRINOSAUR.

Shake 7

For a moment rare
They looked at it there
With its antique glance
And its three-pronged stance,
And from hill to hill
All the folk stood still
As the trino vast
From the living past
Seemed to stare
    And glare
      And leer
        And peer
          And glint
            And squint
Both here and there
From its crystal lair.

Though its head not a mite
    Moved to left nor right,

Its eye seemed to follow you
      Everywhere
  With expression strange
  That seemed to change
    With the shifting
        Drifting
    Light of day.

And it looked at them all
      As if to say,
  'Good afternoon —
    I'm yesterday.'

Shake 8

But the Mayor, Mayoress and party,
   (Appetites distinctly hearty)
      Soon recovered their composure once again,

With their nervous systems doubly
   Fortified by lots of bubbly
      As the waiters handed everyone champagne.

With a sip and then a nibble
   Lord Elastic, Lady Sybil,
      And the others chattered like the monkeys do.

You and I'd not like to be 'em
   In that trinosaur museum
      As it hotter
      hotter
      hotter
      hotter grew.

But it wasn't the bubbly
(As some people vowed)
It wasn't all the fancy clothes,
It wasn't the crowd.

It wasn't the weather
(Though it WAS a trifle trying),
Nor Bill the boiler-man who sent
The temperature high-skying.

It was hotter than Vesuvius
Hotter than the sand,
Hotter than the sun
In a southern land;

Hotter than the red rocks
Underneath the sea,
Hotter than the jungle
Where the trino used to be.

It wasn't Billy Boiler's fault
The switches all stuck.
He stood and scratched his sorry head,
Said,
'Just
my
luck.'

Shake 9

But little Sammy Smother
   Who was standing with his mother
      Just outside the town museum at the time,

Was emitting little cries of
   Joy at all the wheres and whys of
      The great trino as it stood there so sublime,

When quite suddenly he gasped
   And his mother's hand he clasped,
      And in manner hushed and horrified he said,

'I don't *think* that I'm mistaken
   – And I'm feeling rather shaken –
      But I'm SURE I saw the MONSTER MOVE its HEAD!'

'Sammy Smother,' said his ma,
  'It's a wicked boy you are
    Trying hard to spread such panic and confusion –'

'Bless my soul!' said little Sam,
  'It's just winked an eye now, mam.
    I just KNOW it AIN'T an OPTICAL ILLUSION.'

And it wasn't said in fun,
  For the trino had begun
    In all that extra heating to revive,

And the rather special clay
  Of the jungle where it lay
    Had preserved it
      NINETY MILLION YEARS
        ALIVE!

Shake 10

The ceiling

                    shivered

The floor-boards

                    quivered

The boiler

                    belched

And the nuts all

                    squelched

The stairs were

                    smashed

And the pebbles

                    dashed

The carpets

                    rumpled

And the concrete

                    crumpled

The balloons all

                    popped

And the flags all

                    flopped

And shocked and

                    shattered

The people

        S C A T T E R E D

As the whole town

        rang

        With a

        crash

        CRASH

        BANG!

Shake 11

Folk were filled with such surprise
  They could scarce believe their eyes
    (If they hadn't seen it they'd have needed proof)

And they turned distinctly pale
  As the trino wagged its tail
    And removed (quite accidentally) the roof.

As it turned so slowly round
  Several walls fell to the ground
    (One imagines it was feeling rather stiff),

And it flexed a fearsome claw
  And to everybody's awe
    Gave the top of the gasometer a sniff.

Then it drained the waters cool
  Of the Priory Paddling Pool
    And with an ease incredible to see,

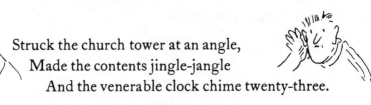

Struck the church tower at an angle,
  Made the contents jingle-jangle
    And the venerable clock chime twenty-three.

Through the windows and the doors
  And the ceiling and the floors
    And the multitude of spaces in between,

Every citizen and guest
  Joined the rout with all the rest
    And retreated in a panic from the scene.

From a distance safe and wise
   People watched and rubbed their eyes
      At a sight not seen since very long B.C.,

And the beast to Borough Square
  Gave a prehistoric air
    As it chewed up fifty bushes and a tree.

Then it sank down in a heap
    And it promptly fell asleep.
        O its fearful snores astounded one and all!

(Though the music had no title
    It was like a loud recital
        On the organ at the Royal Albert Hall.)

Said the Mayor, 'This isn't pretty –
    I must form a small committee
        Till the Services assistance to us send,

'For the Air Force isn't free
    And the Navy's all at sea,
        And the Army's on manoeuvres this weekend.'

So His Worship made his pick,
    Called a meeting double-quick
        At a very secret, hush-hush rendezvous.

Said, 'This situation fierce
    Doesn't call for *volunteers* –
        Which is why I asked for
            you
                and
                    you
                        and
                            you.'

Shake 12

There was Alastair Disaster
    Once a grammar school headmaster
        And whose Latin verse was said to be inspired,

And Miss Esmeralda Flight
    The well-known toxophilite,
        And Wing Commander Wallaby (Retd).

There was Leading Seaman Noggin
    Who'd been years upon the oggin,*
        Stanley Sparks the Captain of the Fire Brigade.

There was dear old Dr Query
    And his friend Father O'Leary,
        And the local undertaker, Mr Spade.

There was Mrs Wheeler-Bent
    Who had stood for Parliament,
        Walter Wave, who'd swum the Channel rather
        slowly,

Sergeant Stripe (who'd borne and grinned it
    Out in Burma as a Chindit)
        And Bernie Ball, the famous England goalie,

With the landlord, Percy Quart
    Who with guns was quite a sport,
        They assembled in the cellar of 'The Boar',

* The sea

And the air was filled with questions
And some rather wild suggestions
When they heard
a knock
Like **THUNDER**
on the door.
They thought it was the trinosaur
The huge and handsome trinosaur
A-knocking on and blocking
(Surely couldn't be *unlocking*?)
In a manner rather shocking
The entrance to their hideaway
(They hoped that it would stride away
Or gracefully would glide away)
A-bumping   grumping   thumping
At their secret cellar door.

But Leading Seaman Noggin
– After just a little sippers* –
(He'd a bottle with some grog in)

Crept as quietly as quiet
Like a shadow on a diet
In his naval-issue slippers

And with not a jar or jolt
Turned the handle, slid the bolt,
Like the others, certain sure
That the knocks they heard before
Were coming from the trino,
From the tri – no – saur.

* Rum

With a simply awful THWACK
Suddenly the door flew back

(Making everybody blench
And their brows with terror drench)

And with somewhat hasty gait
And the words, 'Sorry I'm late,'

Came Professor Cyril Stench
(Chairman of the Local Bench),
Fellow of an Oxford college
And possessing quite a smattering
Of scientific knowledge
(His friends were more than flattering),

Said, 'When I saw the trino
Prancing round just like a rhino
It was clear as clear as clear as clear to see
That the one man in the nation
Who could save a situation
Fast approaching devastation,
And perhaps civilization,
(Please excuse self-commendation)
was
unquestionably,
definitely,
ME.

'So I took a taxi-cab,
Notes I simply had to grab
From a locker in my lab.

Up the stairs with leap and bound!
Scientific studies found!

Observations
Notes
        and data
All corrections
        and errata,

And – among them all – HOORAY!

What we need
to

WIN THE DAY.'

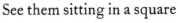

Shake 13

See them sitting in a square

Fireman

   bowman

      goalie

         mayor

Doctor

   undertaker

      preacher

Soldier

   sailor

      airman

         teacher

Channel-swimmer,

   Licensee,

      And the would-have-been M.P.,

Following closely as they can
   The Professor's MASTER-PLAN.

'My idea,' says the Professor as among his notes he delves,
'Is that those of us in Dunborough should deal with this
   OURSELVES.
We could shoot it as it slept, of course, but that would be barbaric,
We could chase it to the River Drown and sink it like a carrack,

'We could drop a rock upon it from the top of the church tower,
Or send harpoons and javelins and arrows in a shower,
There are COUNTLESS ways UNCIVILIZED – of these I
   need not speak –

But I feel we should PRESERVE IT, for the creature is unique:
And it seems to me quite obvious that what we have to do
Is to capture and present it to a Very Special Zoo.

As it slumbers there so sweetly in its grassy green abode – O
   implore you to remember just what happened to the dodo,
And before you're swayed this way or that by military talk,
Fellow citizens, remember the sad fate of the great auk.

SO

While the trino's sleeping now as deep as in a trance
   We'll try a small experiment

               while we have got the chance!'

Shake 14

'Observe,' the good Professor said,
    'That here I have a phial
Of rather special liquid gas
    I want to put on trial.

'I've only just invented it
    For use in zoos and circuses
Upon ALL KINDS OF ANIMALS
    For VETERINARY purposes.

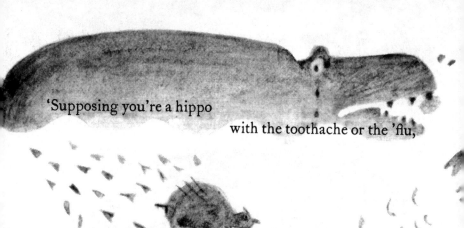

'Supposing you're a hippo
with the toothache or the 'flu,

A hedgehog with the prickly heat,
a jumpy kangaroo,

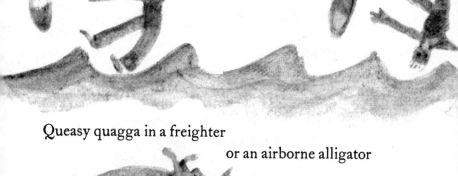

Queasy quagga in a freighter
or an airborne alligator

Or a jackal with a crackle
or a rather nervous gnu.

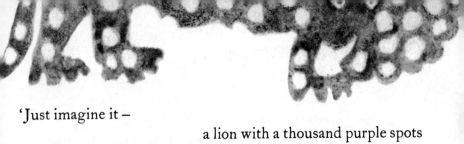

'Just imagine it –

a lion with a thousand purple spots

Or a zebra with no dashes

but with quite a lot of dots,

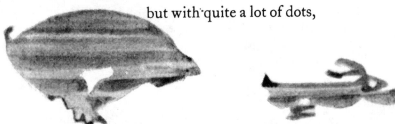
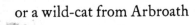

A much-too lively sloth

or a wild-cat from Arbroath

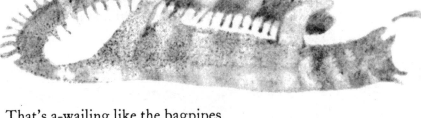

That's a-wailing like the bagpipes
at the Edinburgh Tattoo.

And fancy it – a honey-bear

who's in an awful jam,

A foaming homing-pigeon,

coos, 'I don't know where I am.'

A giraffe with swollen glands

or a camel short of sands,

A cuckoo who can only say

'Tu whit' and then 'Tu whu',

Or a bird who wonders if it's cock-a-one
Or cockatoo.

'For such moments quite distressing
                    I decided it was pressing
To produce a simple remedy
                    Sensationally new,
(Effective, easy, safe AND cheap)
                    to send a creature fast asleep
For anything up to a week
                    and maybe even two.

'And, my friends, only last night
                    As the moon was losing light
And my head was pounding
                    very like a drum,
Round the lab, quite frantic, pacing
                    with my brainbox fairly racing
I was tearing at my hair
                    Absolutely in despair
That the answer I was chasing
                    Wasn't there,

                    WHEN
Just like a flash so bright
                    the solution came in sight
                    as

Shake 15

'That this knockout of a gas

          every other will surpass

Is apparent to me

          more and more and more,

Which is why I've brought you some

          in this jolly little drum

That I found in my

          laboratory store.

And I know with joy you'll jump

          at this hose-pipe and this pump

And the chance to try it on

          THE TRINOSAUR.

'According to my many calculations

          you will find

That the gas has NO EFFECT AT ALL

          upon the HUMAN kind,

But I think that I should warn you

          – or we might get in a pickle –

That the trino's hide is touchy

          at the slightest slap or tickle.

So cautiously we'll climb its tail

                (a very careful track)

And navigate the many bumps

                we see along its back.

THIS portion of its body

                has NO FEELING, I declare,

So it's more or less quite certain

                that it won't know we are there,

And three of us along its spine

                quite peacefully will pass

With stirrup-pump

        and length of hose

                and cylinder of gas.

And when we get right to its head

                of curious shape and size,

Our leader hanging upside-down

                between its sleeping eyes,

As SOON as we've the SIGNAL

                from the fellow with the hose

PROFESSOR STENCH'S SWILIUM

                we'll shoot right up its nose.

'O the trino it will slumber
    And the trino it will snore
Though the Army doesn't get here
    For another month or more.

'And just in case the citizens
    Should fuss and fume and fret
We'll proceed to trap the trino
    Underneath the strongest net.

'And night and day we'll guard it there
    Both lovingly and close
And every time it stirs we'll give it
    Just another dose.

'And when the trino wakens
    And is feeling good as new
We'll present it with the freedom
    Of the latest,
        greatest,
            zoo.'

Shake 16

Plan you gave us —   *bound to save us* —

You're a wonder!   cried the Mayor.

Said mine host,   *Don't want to boast* —

Always thought   *you'd brains to spare.*

Said Miss Flight,   *How very bright!*

Soldier,   *Boys, we've got it made!*

It's a clicker,   said the vicar.

Very deep,   said Mr Spade.

Man's a master,   said Disaster.

Super duper.   (Wheeler-Bent),

Rich and rare, man,   said the airman,

And the swimmer,   *Heaven-sent!*

Agree wholly!   called the goalie,

Said the Doctor,   *It's five-star!*

Oh what larks!   cried Fireman Sparks,

And *Splice the mainbrace!* piped Jack Tar.

Shake 17

No delaying (needs no saying)
    Each one volunteers his aid.
'Not a doubt,' says the Professor,
    Of such stuff are heroes made.

'But the spear-head of the Oper-
    Ation Trino calls for three.
Therefore, Fireman Sparks, ex Leading Seaman
    Noggin
    FOLLOW ME.'

One with pump and one with hose-pipe,
    One with cylinder of gas,
Tip-toed up to where the trino
    Snored as if its lungs were brass.

On the way they found a ladder
    Lying by a garden wall.
Now they've neared the Sports Pavilion!
    Through the hedge-gap see them crawl!

On the creature's rear advancing
Party takes a steady course,
Through the buttercups and daisies
And *a patch of prickly gorse.*

All the citizens of Dunborough
    To their houses were confined,
Though some squinted through a shutter
    Or a chink in window-blind,

While concealed behind the gas-works
Stood the Mayor and his crew
Armed with nets and pegs and mallets,
All prepared to die (or do).

Now the trio leans the ladder
    Gently on the trino's tail.
('Never thought I'd,' Fireman Sparks sighed,
    'Ever work on such a scale.')

As the trino they're ascending,
   Wriggling from bump to bump,
'Blowed if this,' says Seaman Noggin,
   'Don't give me the blooming hump.'

And the watchers in amazement
Looks incredulous exchange,
As they see the careful climbers
On the living mountain-range.

Underneath them in its slumber
– Undisturbed by jig or jog –
Trino sounds like ship on Humber
Snoring homeward through the fog.

Now the Fireman's hanging downwards
  — O what dizziness he feels! —
While above him the Professor
  Holds him tightly by the heels.

(Hanging upside-down between its
  Eyes of very ancient hue,
Fireman can't forbear to wonder
  If it wakes just what he'll do.)

Noggin's pumping! Gas goes thumping!
  (All is well, the trio thinks.)
Says Professor, 'Trino — bless her —
  Out for 40,000 winks.

'When its breath comes slow – then slower
     – Very close watch we must keep –
Is the sign the trino's sinking
     Into
          deep
               and
                    deeper
                         sleep.'

But – mistake in calculation –
     – Poor Professor was aghast –
For instead of breathing slower
     Trino now was breathing fast.

Breathing quick and ever quicker
     Till it gave a loud
                    HICCOUGH!
'Mercy me', exclaimed Professor,
     'But I think it's waking up!'

'Great sea-cats!' called Seaman Noggin,
     'But I'm certain sure that I'll
Soon be wishing I was missing
     From the back of this reptile.'

'Found the reason!' cried Professor.
     'Dreadful error I behold!
SWILIUM FOR *WARM-BLOODED*
     CREATURES!
AND THE TRINOSAUR'S IS
                    COLD!'

'Gas – cold-blooded creatures – wakens
– Plan abandoned – fearful flaw!
Seems to me it would be best to
Rather rapidly WITHDRAW.'

Shake 18

Then all at once the trinosaur
Emitted just the kind of roar
You might have thought had echoed o'er
Some distant prehistoric shore:

Though scholars great and scholars small
Insist such creatures NEVER bawl
Or even as an infant squall
Or make the slightest sound at all –

The fact remains that up till then
The beast was quite beyond the ken
Of scientific modern men,

Who understandably would hum
And say, 'OF COURSE the creature's dumb'

Or on the other hand may haw
And say, 'It's silent, we're quite sure.'

But this conclusion was absurd
In Dunborough
Where its cry
WAS HEARD.

And hear it did our heroes three
As through the town for all to see
Professor, Fireman, Jolly Jack –
Away they galloped on its back.

Yes – off went the trinosaur
        and through the little town it tore
    Just like a puppy off a lead in great exhilaration;
It whirled and waved its tail about,
        (you should have seen it flail about!)
    A-flattening the fir-trees in the Dunborough
        Plantation.

There simply was no stopping it,
        The gallant three still topping it,
    As on the Borough Bowling Green it left a giant
        spoor.
And oh it hopped and skipped and jumped,
        against the Castle wall it bumped
    And made it more a ruin than it ever was before.

Shake 19

It scattered cows,
   It scattered swine,
      It chased a goods-train up the line
         And through the supermarket took a stroll.

On the Castle Green it wandered
   And it chewed the Borough Standard
      As it fluttered on a newly-painted pole.

And the trino seemed QUITE GLUM
   That nobody else would come
      As it rambled and it gambolled here and there,

So as if to keep its pecker up
  It bent a double-decker up
    That happened to be standing in the Square.

On the practice-room it sat,
  Squashed the instruments all flat
    Of the Borough Silver Jubilee Brass Band,

And as up the hill it sprinted
  In the cinema it squinted
    (It's a blessing that no matinée was planned).

Through the reservoir it splashed
As the park-attendants dashed
Like a little herd of goats upon a mountain,

Then it suddenly reversed
And began to quench its thirst
In the Victory Illuminated Fountain.

As it gobbled up a snack
From a rather large haystack
That down beside the water-meadows lay,

It whistled and it wheezed
    And immediately sneezed
        And blew every single wisp of it away.

Said the Mayor to his platoon,
    'We must take some action soon
        Or those three will think our duty we are shirking,

'For I'm certain and I'm sure
    Riding on that trinosaur
        'S an experience that's really rather irking.'

But suggestions there were none
    (For 'twas simpler said than done)
        And our heroes' chances seemed not worth a dime,

When –
refusing to be baffled –
    All three leapt off on a scaffold
        That was round the Baptist Chapel at the time.

O you should have heard the cheer
    That from Dunborough rang clear
        As without a single mutter or a murmur,

That indomitable trio
    With considerable brio
        Descended once again on terra firma.

'My dear friends,' then said the Mayor,
'You have given us a scare
And we're *so* relieved to see you safely down,

'But one fact I must deplore –
We're just where we were before
With that beast still gallivanting round the town.

'Though the danger won't be ended
Till the trino's apprehended
– And such a task the Army's not afraid of –

'I've the feeling still, I own,
We should deal with it ALONE
And show the world what
DUNBOROUGH
is made of!'

Shake 20

Then all at once Miss Flight
  That well-known toxophilite
    With extraordinary luck
      By a sudden thought was struck
        And with flashing eye and bright
          (Quite a formidable sight)
            Straight before His Worship stood
            Like a female Robin Hood.

Said, 'You have no need, I know,
  Of my arrow and my bow –
    From our vow we cannot swerve
      Such a creature to *Conserve*.
        Though in former days, I'm sure,
          They'd have *Killed* that trinosaur
          It would really be unkind
            Not to *Save* it for *Mankind*.

'Though it seems *Complete* reliance
  Can't be placed on modern *Science*,
    And, I feel, a charm or spell
      Somehow wouldn't work too well,
        Long ago it was habitual
          To perform an *Ancient Ritual*.

'And this often was a saviour –
    From such dragonish behaviour
        As the flattening of a city
            Quite without remorse or pity –
                Traffic veering – horses rearing –
                    Herds of cattle disappearing –
                        Pitches generally queering –
                            Every single person fearing!

'Possibly,' said Esmeralda
    As if something strange compelled her,
        'It may prove *No Panacea*
            Yet
                I *think*
                    I've an
                        IDEA!'

People thought their ears deceived,
    Looked incredibly relieved.
        Cried the Mayor, with hope new-springing,
            To the very last straw clinging,
                'Dearest madam, be so kind –
                    Tell us what is in your mind.'

                        '*The Performance of a Rite*',
                            Said Miss Esmeralda Flight.

Shake 21

Yes, up spoke Esmeralda Flight
   As boldly as a gun,
Though sixty summers she had seen
   If she had seen but one.

'Although I must confess,' she said,
   'The prospect isn't nice,
Our last resort that beast to thwart
   Is by a *Sacrifice*.

'For I've been told, in days of old,
   They'd calm a monster down
By offering a virgin maid
   That *she* might save a town.

'And after it had chewed her up
   And all its tribute got –
The beast (quite tame) from whence it came
   Returned, as like as not.

'Though from *Appeasement*, on the whole,
   I wish that we forbore –
If it beguiled a *Dragon* wild,
   Why not a trinosaur?'

The Mayor then said, and shook his head,
  'It's very plain to see
Not one you'll find in her right mind
  That sacrifice to be.

'We wouldn't spoil your plan to foil
  The trino cool and clever,
But – let it sup a lady up
  To save our skins?
        Why –
          NEVER.

'And if for want of human flesh
  It thinner gets and thinner,
That beast SHAN'T munch a maid for lunch
  Or breakfast,
        tea,
          or dinner.'

      But clearly Esmeralda Flight
        With this could not agree,
      For she replied with simple pride,
        That Sacrifice I'll be.

'And I shall dress in lily-white
    And brush and braid my hair,
And bear a posy red and blue
    Upon the morning air.

'A verse or two I'll then recite
    Out of an ancient ode,
And I shall sing an antique song
    That's in the Dorian mode.'

(Then whispered Seaman Noggin, 'Boys,
    Although I ain't no quitter –
I can't conceal this time I feel
    Quite sorry for that crittur.

'When Esmeralda sings and spouts
    And trino frowns above her,
And she draws near in all that gear,
    I think we'd best take cover.')

But though the Mayor and all folk there
    Implored her to relent,
Clear as the sun Miss Esme on
    Self-sacrifice was bent.

'That no-one here's the slightest fear
    Is perfectly well-known,
But – I entreat – that beast *I'll* meet
    And deal with all *alone*.

'So do not flurry, homeward hurry
    With a gentle tread,
And draw the blind, and when you've dined,
    Go early all to bed.

'And bolt the door both aft and fore
    – It really is a must –
And sleep as sound, all eiderdowned,
    As do, I'm told, the just.

'And when my deed of daring's done
    Then let the poets write
She did it all for Dunborough,'
    Said Esmeralda Flight.

Shake 22

But none of the townsfolk
A morning watch kept
For the whole population
It slept and it slept.
The people they slumbered
The clock round about
By all their adventures
Completely worn out,
And long after sun-up
In bed they still lay
And quite unaware
Of the dawn of the day.

When at the Mayor's mansion
In Dockacre Dell
There sounded a sudden
Great ring on the bell,
And O such a knocking
Was heard on the door
The Mayor from his bed
Almost fell on the floor.
'I'm all of a ferment
And flutter, I swear,'
To the Lady Mayoress
Said His Worship the Mayor.

'That dreadful commotion,'
She said, ' I decry,'
As she slowly and solemnly
Opened an eye.
'Though just what's the reason
I vow and declare
I haven't a notion,
And don't really care.
But I've got a feeling
Disaster's not far.
If you ask my advice
You'll stay right where you are.'

But hard upon the window-pane
 A fist of pebbles flew
  And someone on the knocker beat
  A violent tattoo,
   And loudly as the siren sounds
    Upon the Dunborough Brewery
   They heard a most exasperated
    Cry of female fury.
     At once His Worship recognized
      That tone of voice commanding,
     And like a bolt out of his bed
      Shot straight along the landing.

He hurried swiftly down the stair,
  The door he fast unlocked,
  He'd only his pyjamas on
  But nobody was shocked,
    For there with crown of flowers askew
    And hair a sorry sight,
    And virgin gear in state severe
    Stood Esmeralda Flight.
      And all about the Square the Mayor
      With anxious eye did peer
      In case the tricky trinosaur
      Was bringing up the rear.

        But to his relief
        – He could almost have cheered –
        Upon the horizon
        No trino appeared,
          And he cried, 'Dear Miss Flight
          From the beast are you fleeing?
          Please say that it's you –
          Not a ghost that I'm seeing.
          From this world I had feared
          You were gone in great glory –
          Do please come inside
          And tell us your story.'

Said Miss Flight then to the Mayor
   As she sank into a chair
   And consumed a cup of coffee
   With a very thankful air,
      'I'd have never guessed a monster
      – O so fickle and so skittish –
         Would behave in such a manner
         So entirely un-British.
            When I found it snoring loudly
            By the Pennygillam Wood
            I approached it very softly
            As tradition says one should.

'But as I stood before it
   In my ribbons and my train,
      It opened up an eye and then
      It Went to Sleep Again.
         And when my verse I chanted
         At the breaking of the dawn,
            It blinked the other eye and gave
            The most tremendous yawn.
               As slowly I gyrated
               At the coming of the day,
                  Its tail it swished as if it wished
                  That I Would Go Away.

'Though long before its jaws I stood
And offered up my flowers,
It took one peep – then fell asleep
For hours and hours and hours,
And when I offered up *Myself*
It gave a sort of shiver
And caught my posy in a claw
And flung it in the river.
And then my sacrificial robe
It seized with fearful grip,
And dumped me very gently
On the Corporation Tip.

'I shouldn't be complaining –
   But oh, it isn't nice
   When such a beast refuses
   A maiden's sacrifice.
      Right to the heart it's cut me
      Like the sharpest kitchen-knife.
      I've never been insulted
         Quite like this *In All My Life.*'
         And O her eye it flashed as bright
         As Longships or Nantucket,
            And then her tears began to fall
            Enough to fill a bucket.

The Mayor and Mayoress hastened
   With their tissues and their hankies
   And the atmosphere resounded
      With their 'Much obliged's and 'Thank'ee's
      As they voiced to Esmeralda
      In her sacrificial vesture
         ALL the thanks of ALL the people
         For her brave and noble gesture.
            'In the whole of Dunborough's history,'
            They said, 'There's none to match you,
            We'll surely need to mark your deed
            By plaque or bust or statue.

'For we thought by now, dear lady,
  You'd have surely been a goner
  Which is why we'll try and do you
  The most special, signal honour.'
    So Esmeralda's spirits rose
    Considerably higher,
      And all around the floor and ground
      Became a little drier.
        'And now,' His Worship said, 'before
        I go completely barmy,
        Just one thing more:
          THAT TRINOSAUR
            WE'RE LEAVING TO THE ARMY.

'And when the troops they come to town
  — In all the world, none better! —
  The trino's skin ain't worth a pin
  (That's if they got my letter).
    In military tactics they'll
    Be anything but lacking,
      And very soon they'll change its tune
      And send that creature packing.
        I say it once, I say it twice,
        — Let none my words be scorning —
        That trinosaur will be no more
          AS OF NEXT MONDAY
          MORNING.'

Shake 23

But early Monday morning
      With the coming of the dawn,
Young Sammy Smother through the town
      Ran crying out,
                  'IT'S GAWN!

'I got up very early
      And I searched just everywhere –
I rubbed my eyes! To my surprise
      It simply wasn't there!

'It's been and gone and scarpered
      And it's left us in a funk!
Now who'd have thought the trino
      Would have done a blessed bunk?'

At Sammy's shout the people
      Came springing from their beds,
And from the doors and windows
      Soon were sticking out their heads.

'Oh, it's Sammy!'
                        'Where's your mammy?'
'*What* was that we heard you say?'
'Trino's missing?'
                        'Oh, how spiffing!'
'Just imagine it!'
                  'HOORAY!'

And the citizens of Dunborough
    They looked hither, they looked yon,
But they found to their astonishment
    The trinosaur was gone.

It wasn't on the hillside
    And it wasn't on the down,
It wasn't in the meadows
    Down beside the River Drown.

It wasn't in the Priory Park,
    It wasn't in the pool,
It wasn't in the playground
    Of the Church of England school.

Both street and square were free as air
    Of any beast-ly bother,
For in the town it wasn't found
    From one end to the other.

That all the folk were puzzled
    There was not the slightest doubt.
They said, 'This is a mystery
    We really can't make out.'

When,
    'I've got it!' cried Disaster
  (Once headmaster) to the Mayor
 (Spoke so sharply that His Worship
    Leapt a little in the air).

'It only now occurred to me
   – The very strangest thing! –
When looking at the calendar –
   Today's the FIRST OF SPRING!

'And on this day the birds and beasts
   – So ancient lore relates –
Go searching here and searching there
   To find themselves their mates.

'And THAT is why the trinosaur
   Is swimming in the foam
From east to west to its love-nest
   Back in its jungle-home.

'Of finding mates in Dunborough
   A trino's not much hope –
It clearly needs a wider sphere
   And somewhat larger scope.'

You should have heard the people
   Make such a hullabaloo!
They hadn't felt so happy
   Since the end of World War II.

They laughed and sang and shouted,
   With joy their faces shone,
To think at last from Dunborough
   The trinosaur had gone.

But as they clapped and capered
    And joyful cheers were sounding,
A figure from the riverside
    To Borough Square came pounding.

'Your Worship! Oh, Your Worship!'
    Yelled Sammy Smother's brother
'You know we *lost* one trinosaur?
    Well, now we've got ANOTHER!'

'Such dreadful news,' declared the Mayor,
  'Makes me feel cold and clammy.
Is that the truth he's telling us?
  Please ask young Simmy, Sammy.'

Said Sim, 'That it's a trino
  Is obvious – alack –
And so's the DOUBLE row of bumps
  I saw upon its back.'

'A DOUBLE ROW?' cried Noggin,
  'Why then, it's plain to see:
This time it ain't a female
  But the opposite – a HE.

'And as he's swimming UP the Drown
  – Now don't forget the date! –
He's searching for a partner
  And he's just a little late.

'Although I'll lay with love his eye
  Burns like a lump of cannel,
By fate's sad twist his mate he's missed
  While in the English Channel.'

When to the highest hilltop
   The citizens had sped
They saw the trino swimming
   As little Sim had said.

In the white morning sunlight
   It looked so very striking –
Its figurehead and rudder
   Like the vessel of a Viking.

But that it swam for love and peace
   And never swam for war
Was clear as was the water
   About that trinosaur.

And through the river-valley
   They watched the trino go,
And up above the trees its head
   Move gently to and fro.

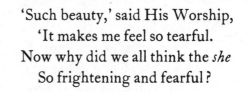

'Such beauty,' said His Worship,
   'It makes me feel so tearful.
Now why did we all think the *she*
   So frightening and fearful?

'Although it broke up floors and doors
   And sheds and beds and ceilings,
It's clearer now – one should allow
   For trinos' FINER FEELINGS.

'In all the world it's certain,
   Few creatures have such charm,
And – come to think of it – it did
   No-one the SLIGHTEST harm.'

(To hear them talking you'd have thought
   That every mother's son
Was eager to have trino two
   As well as trino one.)

But observations of this kind
   Were rapidly cut short
When from afar there came a Sound
   Of Sinister Import.

They heard loud squeals from tyres and wheels
    On missiles quite appalling,
And Non-Commissioned Officers
    A-bellowing and bawling.

All up and down the steeps the jeeps
Were hooting and were humming,
And trucks and lorries by the score
Gave many a rattle and a roar
As if to say,

                              'O trinosaur

The Army's
    coming
        COMING.'

They'd umpteen different kinds of gun
And ammunition by the ton
Including bomb and shell and mine
And booby-traps of dread design,
And, camouflaged in blue and green,
Of aspect menacing and mean,
The very first one ever seen,

A military submarine

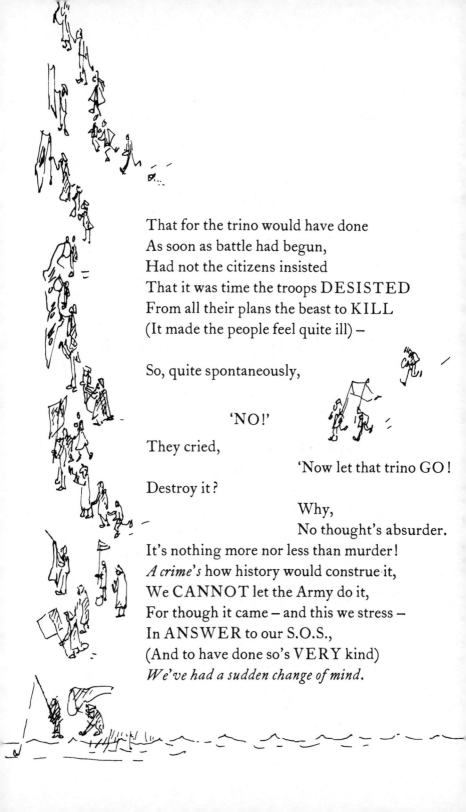

That for the trino would have done
As soon as battle had begun,
Had not the citizens insisted
That it was time the troops DESISTED
From all their plans the beast to KILL
(It made the people feel quite ill) –

So, quite spontaneously,

'NO!'

They cried,

'Now let that trino GO!

Destroy it?

Why,
No thought's absurder.
It's nothing more nor less than murder!
A crime's how history would construe it,
We CANNOT let the Army do it,
For though it came – and this we stress –
In ANSWER to our S.O.S.,
(And to have done so's VERY kind)
We've had a sudden change of mind.

Shake 24

'Far better,'
        they said,
            'that we help if we can
The trino to live out its natural span,
And not out of malice or simply for sport
Its life here on earth for a second cut short.
The soldiers will think we are greener than grass
If all we can think of is,
                "THEY SHALL NOT PASS!"
(Such slogans would seem to them terribly rum
For, if you remember, WE ASKED them to COME).

'Yes, it's clear as the sign on the side of a bus
A trino's a place on this planet – like us,
And all of a sudden it's plain as can be
It's part of creation, like you and like me.

'WE COULDN'T expose it (too painful the topic!)
To gaggles of gunners with sights telescopic.
It'd scare the poor creature clean out of its wits
If the Royal Artillery blew it to bits.
So let's go together to Watergate Street,
And try and persuade it to beat a retreat.'

The folk to the river then ran in a throng

To the spot where the trino was swimming along –
A picture so peaceful of primeval bliss
As it waved its head happily that way and this.

But seeing the crowd that appeared on the verge
It put on its brakes and prepared to submerge
(A move, come to think of it, childish and callow –
The river just here was decidedly shallow),

And what with the people, including the Mayor,
All leaping,
      and pointing,
            and shouting,

'TAKE CARE!'

The trinosaur, looking a trifle perplexed,
Seemed rather uncertain as what to do next,
And in its sad eyes two great tears seemed to quiver
As if to say,
    'WHY
        are they pointing down-river
With stick and umbrella and finger and thumb?
How VERY unfriendly –
          I've only just come –
If you're cross that I'm late –
         Well, I caught the first tide—
And ALL that I'm seeking's a trinosaur bride.'

With fears for its safety now seaward they pointed,
The whole river-bank with directions anointed,
Waved SHEETS on which ARROWS they'd
  HASTILY PAINTED
That with its escape-route the beast was acquainted –

When, loud as a thunder-stroke, clear as a flash,

Right into its brain-box

their message
fell
CRASH:

And it turned
ROUNDABOUT
with a whirl and a splash,
And soon beyond range of the shells and the shots
It swam for the sea at a fast rate of knots,
First pausing to give to the crowd on the banks
A nod of its head just as if to say
thanks.

Then up to the town ran the folk from the creek,
  Delighted the trino was saved – by a squeak;
And puffing and bluffing (and hiding a grin)

They waved and they cheered as the Army came in.

'Good day,' said the General. 'Jolly bad show.
     Leave that tiresome trino to us, doncherknow.'

But O with a charmingly innocent air,
     'Better never than late,' said His Worship the Mayor.

THE COUNTRY CHILD
Alison Uttley

THE CUCKOO CLOCK
Mrs Molesworth

THE ELEPHANT WAR
Gillian Avery

THE HOUSE IN NORHAM GARDENS
Penelope Lively

THE LITTLE DUKE
Charlotte Yonge

THE ORDINARY PRINCESS
M.M. Kaye

THE PIRATES IN THE DEEP GREEN SEA
Eric Linklater

THE TWELVE AND THE GENII
Pauline Clarke

THE WIND ON THE MOON
Eric Linklater

THE WOODS OF WINDRI
Violet Needham

THE VOYAGE OF QV66
Penelope Lively